ON THE HUNT WITH CROCODILES

BY KRISTEN POPE

The Child's World®
childsworld.com

Published by The Child's World®
1980 Lookout Drive • Mankato, MN 56003-1705
800-599-READ • www.childsworld.com

Acknowledgments
The Child's World®: Mary Berendes, Publishing Director
Red Line Editorial: Design, editorial direction, and production
Photographs ©: Shutterstock Images, cover, 1, 8, 17, 20; Mike Parry/Minden
Pictures/Corbis, 4; Oded Ben-Raphael/Shutterstock Images, 6; Red Line
Editorial, 10; Enrique Ramos/Shutterstock Images, 11; Jordi Prat Puig/
Shutterstock Images, 12; iStockphoto, 14; Sergei Kolesnikov/Shutterstock
Images, 15; Andre Anita/Shutterstock Images, 16; Nigel J. Dennis/NHPA/
Photoshot/Newscom, 18

ISBN 9781634074490

LCCN 2015946263

Printed in the United States of America
Mankato, MN
December, 2015
PA02279

TABLE OF
CONTENTS

Chapter 1
ON THE HUNT 5

Chapter 2
BY THE POND 9

Chapter 3
NILE CROCODILES 13

Chapter 4
CROCODILE BABIES 19

Glossary 22
To Learn More 23
Selected Bibliography 23
Index 24
About the Author 24

ON THE HUNT

The pond is still and quiet. A crocodile walks up to the edge of the water. It slips its body into the pond. Smoothly, it dives under the water. It uses its strong tail and webbed hind feet to swim. Crocodiles are at home in the water. When the crocodile comes up, only its eyes are above the water.

Flies buzz above the water as the crocodile waits. The crocodile is not in any hurry. It can hold its breath underwater for an hour. Even in the water, crocodiles use their senses. Crocodiles can still see and hear underwater. Small slits on their heads lead to their ears. When a crocodile dives underwater, it closes these slits. The closed slits keep the water out of its ears.

Out of the corner of its eye, the crocodile sees a turtle. The turtle walks on dry, stiff leaves near the pond. The crocodile uses the water's cover to move close. Crocodiles have very good eyesight. **Prey** near the water is easy to catch. The prey usually doesn't see the crocodile **predator** until it is too late. The sound

◀ **Crocodiles can swim up to 20 miles (32 km) per hour.**

▲ **With just its eyes above the water, the crocodile is
nearly invisible.**

of crunching leaves gets louder. The sound travels to the small
slits on the crocodile's head and into its ears. The turtle is
moving closer.

The turtle walks up to the edge of the pond. It steps into
the pond. The crocodile feels the water ripple. Even in dark and
dirty water, the crocodile knows what is nearby. The crocodile
closes the slits that lead to its ears. Then, it ducks down into the

water a little more. When the prey is close, the crocodile springs into action.

The crocodile uses its strong tail to build power and speed. It lunges fiercely. With a terrific splash, the crocodile snatches up the turtle. It grabs the animal in its mouth. A crack rings out as the crocodile chomps through the turtle's shell. Crocodiles have the strongest bite of any animal on the planet.

The powerful **carnivore** opens its mouth wide and tosses its head back. About 100 teeth glisten in its mouth. A few new teeth are growing. Even though the crocodile is an adult, it has new teeth. These teeth grow in waves. A crocodile can have 8,000 teeth over its whole lifetime. But it doesn't use its teeth to chew. Crocodiles do not chew their food. They tear off hunks of food. Or they swallow it whole. Their teeth are used to catch their prey.

The massive crocodile shakes its head a few times. It rips off a hunk of turtle. The crocodile throws its head back. It shakes its head up and down. This helps the chunk of meat slide down its throat. This meal will be its only food for the day. It can live for months without eating. When it is time to eat, the crocodile can eat a lot. The turtle was small. But sometimes crocodiles eat half their body weight at one time.

Chapter 2

BY THE POND

A frog lets out a mighty croak. Insects buzz everywhere. Crabs scuttle in the shallow water. This Florida pond is full of life. The crocodile has lots of food to eat at this pond. Sometimes the crocodile eats small animals, such as raccoons, rabbits, birds, fish, crabs, or frogs. In other places, crocodiles will eat bigger animals, such as pigs, deer, or even buffalo. In Africa, Nile crocodiles can eat zebras, wildebeests, and small hippos.

Crocodiles live mostly in Africa and the United States. Some crocodiles live in South America, Asia, and Australia. Crocodiles are not able to run very fast or for long on land. They are much better hunters from the water.

Pulling itself to the shore, the crocodile rests. The lone crocodile is still full from the turtle. Full for now, at least. It sleeps in short naps, usually during the day. The crocodile is always ready to wake up. It never sleeps very deeply. The crocodile lays out

◄ Crocodiles usually stay in or near water, where they are stronger predators.

▲ American and Nile crocodiles live in different parts of the world.

on the muddy shore near the pond. It is 13 feet (4 m) long. This crocodile is an average-sized American crocodile.

It peers across the pond. An alligator is on the other side. Florida is the only place in the world with both alligators and crocodiles. The crocodile and alligator look similar. But the crocodile has a longer snout. It is thinner than the alligator's snout. The crocodile also has teeth sticking out when it closes its mouth. The alligator does not.

Unlike alligators, some of a crocodile's teeth stick out of ▶ its snout.

Chapter 3

NILE CROCODILES

Across the world, a different kind of crocodile waits to eat. The Nile crocodile is on the hunt in Africa. It waits next to a slow-moving river. The water is dark and dirty. The crocodile stretches out on the muddy bank. It is nearly 20 feet (6 m) long. As it moves, its feet sink into the mud. At more than 1,600 pounds (726 kg), this crocodile is massive. It is one of the biggest Nile crocodiles in the world.

The crocodile slips into the water. It swims upstream. A Nile perch swims by the crocodile. The crocodile quickly snaps up the fish. It swallows the perch in one gulp. This small fish is tasty. But it won't be enough to fill the crocodile's stomach. In the distance, a heron lands in the river. Using its strong tail, the crocodile swims farther up the river. Diving down, the crocodile uses its tail to build power and speed. It then rushes to the surface. The crocodile leaps up and out of the water. With its giant jaws, it grabs the bird.

◀ **Nile crocodiles are Africa's largest kind of crocodile.**

▲ **Wildebeests look for a way to cross the water.**

The crocodile notices more prey. This is a busy hunting day. A group of wildebeests carefully walk by the river. They look up and down the river. But they don't notice the crocodile. Each wildebeest weighs around 500 pounds (227 kg). The crocodile will have to use a special hunting technique because its prey is so big. After the wildebeests step into the water, the crocodile makes its move. With one snap of its jaw, the crocodile snatches the closest wildebeest. The shocked animal splashes. But the crocodile pulls the kicking wildebeest underwater. Using this death roll, the crocodile spins the wildebeest under the water.

◀ **Crocodiles use their strong tails to leap out of the water.**

▲ **The crocodile clamps onto its prey.**

There is a giant splash as the two animals struggle. Water flies everywhere. But the crocodile will win this fight. It can hold its breath for an hour. The wildebeest cannot hold its breath nearly as long. The crocodile twirls the wildebeest under the water. The wildebeest struggles. It tries to break free from the crocodile. But the wildebeest soon drowns. The death roll worked again. The crocodile surfaces and drags the wildebeest around in its huge jaw. The other wildebeests are gone. But this one will be a big meal for the crocodile. The crocodile carries its meal to shallower water. It rips off a hunk of meat, flings its head back, and lets the meat slide down its throat.

After its meal, the crocodile lays out on the bank. The African sun is hot. The crocodile opens its mouth to let heat escape. Crocodiles don't have sweat glands, so they open their mouths to cool down. Crocodiles are **reptiles**. They bask in the hot sun to keep themselves warm.

▲ Much like a panting dog, crocodiles leave their mouths open to cool their body temperature.

Chapter 4

CROCODILE BABIES

The Nile crocodile rests at the water's edge. Downriver, another Nile crocodile watches over her nest in the sand. A female Nile crocodile can start laying eggs when she is between 12 and 19 years old. Crocodiles live to be about 70 years old. She can lay eggs once or twice a year. This crocodile guards her 50 or so eggs from hyenas, monitor lizards, and other animals that might eat them. Mothers dig holes, or nests, and lay their eggs in the holes. The eggs are then covered with a thin layer of sandy dirt. This layer helps keep the eggs warm. When sunshine hits the nest, the eggs get toasty warm. The nest is only a few feet from the river. This helps the babies quickly find the water when they hatch.

A faint squeak comes from the eggs. With her excellent hearing, the mother crocodile can hear the babies squeak in their shells. They are ready to hatch. The mother gently unburies her eggs. She can hear one is trying to get out. The baby crocodile uses its **egg tooth** to try to exit its shell. Using the tooth, the baby

◀ **A mother crocodile watches over her nest, which is about 20 inches (50 cm) deep.**

pecks at the shell. But it is not having much luck. It is stuck in the leathery eggshell.

The mother steps in to help. She gently picks up the egg with her mouth. Then she carefully rolls it in her mouth. Slowly, the shell starts to crack. She lowers her mouth. The egg gently rolls back out into the nest. The baby crocodile peeks out. Its shell is almost gone. A few minutes later, the **hatchling** makes its way out.

The mother picks up the hatchling with her mouth. She carries it to the water. Slowly, she opens up her mouth. She lets it go,

▲ **Hatchlings are able to walk right after they hatch out of their eggs.**

and it starts to swim. It looks for insects to eat. She keeps an eye on her baby. But then she hears a noise in the distance. She scoops the baby crocodile up in her mouth. It is safer in there. She heads back to the nest where the other babies are hatching. They also need her help. If the father crocodile is around, he will help guard the nest. Sometimes the mother has to go into the water to cool down. The father watches the nest then. He is very protective of his babies, too.

The mother crocodile hears something in the distance. It is a human. Someone from the nearby town is coming to the river. The mother heads back to her nest. Humans sometimes shoot crocodiles. This human might be looking to kill crocodiles out of fear.

The female crocodile waits, covering her nest. She is ready to defend it. The babies can stay with their mother for up to two years. She will help protect them. Snakes and other animals like to eat baby crocodiles. Sometimes, lions and leopards will eat a small adult crocodile. The human voice heads in a different direction. The mother moves off her nest. She begins helping the hatchlings out of their shells. She helps them break out one by one. A few break out on their own. A new generation of Nile crocodiles is here.

GLOSSARY

carnivore (KAHR-nuh-vor): A carnivore is an animal that eats meat. The crocodile is a carnivore.

egg tooth (eg tooth): An egg tooth is a special tool on each baby crocodile's jaw that helps it to break out of its shell. The baby crocodile uses its egg tooth to peck at its leathery shell from the inside.

hatchling (HACH-ling): A hatchling is a newborn animal that has just come out of its egg. A crocodile hatchling can walk just after hatching.

predator (PRED-uh-ter): A predator is an animal that eats other animals. The crocodile is a fierce predator.

prey (PRAY): Prey are animals that are eaten by other animals. Turtles are the prey of crocodiles.

reptiles (REP-tilez): Reptiles are cold-blooded animals that crawl on their bellies or creep on short legs. Crocodiles, snakes, lizards, and turtles are all reptiles.

snout (snout): A snout is the long front part of an animal's head that includes the nose, mouth, and jaws. A crocodile snout is longer and thinner than an alligator snout.

To Learn More

Books

Calhoun, Kelly. *Scaly Swimmers*. Ann Arbor, MI: Cherry Lake Publishing, 2016.

Herrington, Lisa M. *Crocodiles and Alligators*. New York: Children's Press, 2016.

Tyler, Gemma. *Crocodile*. New York: Bearport Publishing, 2016.

Web Sites

Visit our Web site for links about crocodiles: childsworld.com/links

Note to Parents, Teachers, and Librarians: We routinely verify our Web links to make sure they are safe and active sites. So encourage your readers to check them out!

Selected Bibliography

"American Crocodile." *National Geographic*. National Geographic, n.d. Web. 4 May 2015.

"Basic Facts about Crocodiles." *Defenders.org*. Defenders of Wildlife, 2015. Web. 3 May 2015.

"Nile Crocodile." *Nature.org*. The Nature Conservatory, 2015. Web. 5 May 2015.

"World's Deadliest: Crocs Kill with Strongest Bite." *National Geographic*. National Geographic, n.d. Web. 4 May 2015.

INDEX

alligator, 10

American crocodiles, 10

death roll, 15–16

egg tooth, 19

eggs, 19–20

eyesight, 5

hatchlings, 20–21

length, 10, 13

map, 10

napping, 9

nest, 19–21

Nile crocodiles, 9–21

prey, 5, 7, 15

snout, 10

swimming, 5, 13, 21

tail, 5, 7, 13

teeth, 7, 10

weight, 13

ABOUT THE AUTHOR

Kristen Pope is a writer and editor with years of experience working in national and state parks and museums. She has taught people of all ages about science and the environment, including coaxing reluctant insect-lovers to pet Madagascar hissing cockroaches.